Christ Rhythms was born in th̲ church. For the new Christia̲ ing catalyst for understanding your identity in Christ and following him. For the seasoned believer, it's the tool you've been looking for to help connect others to Christ and his church. Simple, practical, conversational—*Christ Rhythms* is about a one-on-one connection versus a classroom. Whether you're a brand-new believer or a seasoned Christ-follower, you need this book!"

Matt Carter, lead pastor, Sagemont Church, Houston, TX

Plenty of Christians want more in their relationship with Jesus but don't know where to start. *Christ Rhythms* is a really refreshing mixture of Bible, theology, instruction, and application that is sure to help any Christian experience more confidence and joy in following Jesus. I have witnessed the fruit of *Christ Rhythms*. God has and will continue to use its content to cultivate well-rounded, joy-filled, fully devoted disciples of Jesus.

Timothy Ateek, teaching pastor, Watermark Church, Dallas, TX

I am always on the hunt for accessible discipleship resources that anyone can understand and that also spark good conversations in my discipleship relationships. In *Christ Rhythms*, Jonathan provides just that, making it a book

I will be using in my ministry and passing along to other disciple-makers.

Christine Hoover, pastor's wife, author, Bible teacher, and podcaster (christinehoover.net)

Christ Rhythms practically and intellectually presents the intimate nature of a healthy relationship with Jesus Christ. For the new believer it provides a concise theological discipleship tool to begin their journey with Jesus. However, this book is not limited to new believers; rather, it refreshes the foundations of faith for all believers. *Christ Rhythms* was formed with the heart of discipleship, and it is a tool to build healthy believers both in small groups and one-on-one interactions.

Pierre Cannings, dean, Dallas Theological Seminary, Houston campus

JONATHAN BROOKS

Christ Rhythms

A Jumpstart Guide to Life in Christ

Dedication

To the love of my life and my beautiful bride, Stephani. You continually amaze me in the way you pour yourself out for our family and for the sake of the gospel. Without you, I would be a far less sanctified, less gracious follower of Jesus!

To my children, Luke, Levi, Titus, Benjamin, and Ruthie. I long for the day that you are all walking with Jesus, living in the life-giving rhythms of gospel purpose. You bring me such great joy.

To the members of Restoration Church Bryan, whom I have the privilege and joy of leading and shepherding. I pray this book is a blessing and a supplement to the Word of God to help you know and follow Jesus.

Contents

Introduction

Congrats! If you are jumping into this discipleship journey, it's because Jesus has saved you and (Lord willing!) is beginning to transform your life. You have called out to Jesus (Romans 10:13) and placed your faith in his life, death, and resurrection. Whether God saved you ten years ago or ten days ago, hopefully you're pursuing this "life in Christ" because you recognize that pursuing a relationship with Jesus is not only important but also *the* defining purpose of the Christian life.

The Bible

At this point, it's important to recognize a few things. First, thinking about reading the Bible may be overwhelming to you. You may not even know where to begin! In fact, some people start in the Old Testament but then get discouraged and give up after getting a few books in. The Old Testament is immensely important, but it ultimately points ahead and prepares us for the arrival of Jesus in the New Testament. In fact, once you understand the New Testament (Matthew–Revelation), then you can go back and better understand the purpose of the Old Testament.

The Connection and the Process

Second, you may think that Christians and those you run into at church have it all together, that they are all Bible scholars or somehow have a closer connection to God than you. Nothing could be further from the truth. In fact, the Bible tells us in 1 Timothy 2:5: "For there is one God, and one mediator between God and men, the man Christ Jesus." Among other things, this verse says you have the same direct access to God through Jesus as anyone else! Now, that doesn't mean you don't need others to help you grow in your faith. But the truth is *every* Christian is still in process. None of us has arrived. We all still struggle with the presence of sin and brokenness. So here's the encouragement: don't get overwhelmed with where you are, with where you need to grow, or with your perception of others. Just focus on your connection to Jesus.

The Need for Others

This third important point may seem counterintuitive to the second point, but it's necessary and should provide a healthy balance. Though you have direct access to God through Jesus, you still need others to grow. Being a part of God's church is a team sport! And though none of us has the market cornered on a perfect relationship with Jesus, you must seek out mature followers of Jesus to help you grow. For that reason, you *should* find someone to walk with you

> Find someone to walk with you.

through these next eight weeks as you begin your new life in Christ.

As you are on this discipleship journey, each week you'll be looking at four things to help you know and follow Jesus better:

- *A Passage to Dive Into.* Build the habit of daily reading and applying the Bible to your life.
- *A Promise to Deposit.* Take to heart some of the most fundamental promises of God.
- *A Truth to Discover.* Grow in your understanding in some fundamental truths of God.
- *A Habit to Develop.* Begin to take ownership of your faith by building Christian habits.

One more necessary word before you dive in: the heart behind this book is to help provide a "spiritual jumpstart" for Christians. Someone in need of a literal jumpstart already has the vehicle. They also have at least an idea of where they are going. What they need is an external push or power to get the engine firing and the car moving. Though this book is not the end-all-be-all book for discipleship, Lord willing, it will serve as a "primer" to get the momentum going.

So buckle up. Know that following the rhythms of Jesus as you pursue a relationship with him won't be easy, but it's worth it. Let the adventure begin!

Proof of Love

A Passage to Dive Into

Read Mark 1–5 this week.

We recommend reading a chapter each day (Monday–Friday). As you read, ask yourself the following questions:

1. What does this passage reveal about God?
2. What does it reveal about humanity/me?
3. Is there a command of God that I can obey? How can I apply this passage to my life this week? Is there any sin that I need to confess?
4. How does this passage point me to Jesus?

Pointers

- Don't get overwhelmed!
- Pray as you read—ask God to help you understand.
- Highlight what stands out to you.
- If you have questions, write them down!
- As you read, ask if there's something you can apply to your life today.

A Promise to Deposit

You are immeasurably loved by God.

For God so loved the world, that he gave his
only [begotten] Son, that whoever believes in
him should not perish but have eternal life.

John 3:16

Many people are familiar with this verse from the Gospel of John. In fact, a lot of folks just sort of "assume" the love of God as if they are entitled to it! Some think God owes us his love. Others have a high view of themselves and think, *Why wouldn't God love me? After all, I'm pretty awesome!* But the truth of the apostle John's words is much more powerful. In fact, that Greek word for "world" is *kosmos*. This was not a world that had the warm fuzzies for God! This was not even a world that sought after God. Rather, *kosmos* is the world system hell-bent on rebelling against God and undermining his authority. John says God loved *that* world. He loved the broken, sinful, and rebellious one. This is the world into which he sent Jesus.

Romans 5:8 puts it like this: "But God shows his love for us in that while we were still sinners, Christ died for us." This is where God met *you*. Not when you had it all together. Not when you were even seeking after God. Tim

Keller tells us, "The gospel is this: We are more sinful and flawed in ourselves than we ever dared believe, yet at the very same time we are more loved and accepted in Jesus Christ than we ever dared hope."[1]

Wow. This means God saw all your brokenness. He saw all your sin (past, present, and future). He saw you even in your rebellion and unbelief, and he loved you enough to save you. This is why we talk about "amazing grace." Biblical grace, by definition, is undeserved favor. If it was deserved, you would have done something to merit it. But the Bible reveals that God loved you at your worst.

> This means God saw all your brokenness.

Let that sink in for a moment.

You are immeasurably loved by God. If you're looking for proof that God immensely loves you, look no further than the cross of Jesus.

Read Romans 8:35–39. What is the personal significance of this passage to you? Share with the one walking with you through this book.

_____

_____

_____

_____

_____

A Truth to Discover

Jesus is God and the only source of your salvation.

The Bible says Jesus is the only begotten "Son" of the Father. In Week 4 we will cover the biblical concept of a "triune God" or "Trinity." We'll dive further into the truth that God, though one God, exists as the Father, Son, and Holy Spirit.

The Person of Jesus

But what does it mean that Jesus is both "begotten" and a "Son"?

First, Scripture says that Jesus was "begotten," which means not created or fashioned. Yes, Jesus appeared in space and time on this earth—he came in human flesh and was fully man (John 1:14). But there was never a time when Jesus did not exist as God (John 1:1–4). He has always shared the same substance and glory of the Father. This is why Jesus told his disciples, "I and the Father are one" (John 10:30). Throughout history, every cult and religious movement that has gotten off track (and into error) has either diminished Jesus' divinity or his humanity. We must hold both in tension, though obviously we may never fully wrap our minds around the dual nature of Jesus.

What about the term "Son"? For most of us, our only connotation for this word is that of a flesh-and-blood son. However, we must understand and embrace another biblical connotation. "Son" also carries the meaning of "image bearer." Jesus came as a man to give us the perfect picture and exact representation of who God is. (Read Colossians 1:15–20 and discuss.) Though Jesus came in human flesh, he did not cease to be God even though he voluntarily limited himself by taking on the form of a servant (Philippians 2:5–11).

The Work of Jesus

Jesus did many incredible things and performed many amazing miracles (John 20:30–31). He lived a perfect, sinless life (Hebrews 4:15; 2 Corinthians 5:21), something no other person has ever accomplished.

> Ultimately, Jesus came to redeem people (set us free!) from the stronghold of sin and to restore us to a right relationship with God.

He alone is the mediator between God and man (1 Timothy 2:5). In his infinite love for those who were lost and broken, Jesus died as the perfect sacrifice, shedding his blood on a Roman cross for the sins of the world (Luke 24:20). At the cross, Jesus died in our place as a substitute (1 Peter 3:18), the just for the unjust. At the cross both divine justice and mercy were on display as God's penalty for sin was satisfied in Jesus when he gave his life to save us.

But because Jesus was God incarnate and was without sin, death could not hold him. (Death was the sentence reserved for sinners!) Scripture reveals that after three days, Jesus gloriously arose from the dead (Luke 24:6–7), proving to be the victor over both sin and death. Jesus is alive! He later ascended to the Father and is now seated at the Father's right hand (John 20:17). Jesus, as our forerunner (Hebrews 6:20), has gone before us in life, death, and resurrection.

He is sovereign over all things and is the Head of his bride, the church. As our High Priest, he now intercedes (as the perfect intermediary between God and humanity) for us (Hebrews 7:24). He alone is the source of our life, our wisdom, righteousness, sanctification, and redemption (1 Corinthians 1:30). Jesus is worthy of our praise, adoration, affections, devotion, and obedience. He is Lord. The Bible reveals that one day Jesus will return (Titus 2:13), and he will make all things right, bringing restoration to the entire world (Acts 3:21).

Discussion

1. Go back and discuss the Tim Keller quote. Is your mindset, *Of course, God loves me!* or is it, *How in the world could God love me?* How should the certainty of God's love impact your life?

_____

_____

_____

_____

2. Why is it important to have a biblical understanding
   of who Jesus is (versus fashioning a Jesus of your
   own design)?

_____

_____

_____

_____

_____

3. Do you have any questions about this truth
   to discover?

_____

_____

_____

_____

_____

A Habit to Develop: Baptism

*Read Act 8:34–38; 16:30–34. Discuss the
importance of biblical baptism.*

"Baptizing them in the name of the Father
and of the Son and of the Holy Spirit."

Matthew 28:19

Baptism does not save you, but Jesus does! However, in Matthew 28 Jesus commanded his followers to be baptized. Baptism is a picture of Christ's being buried and raised. It's also a testimony of our new life "in Christ." It is the outward picture of an inward reality (e.g., a wedding ring).

Discuss the importance of baptism. (Yes! This one is less of a "habit" and more of a one-time act of obedience.) Have you taken this step of obedience?

By Grace
Through Faith

A Passage to Dive Into

Read Mark 6–10 this week.

We recommend reading a chapter each day (Monday–Friday). As you read, ask yourself the following questions:

1. What does this passage reveal about God?
2. What does it reveal about humanity/me?
3. Is there a command of God that I can obey? How can I apply this passage to my life this week? Is there any sin that I need to confess?
4. How does this passage point me to Jesus?

Pointers

- Don't get overwhelmed!
- Pray as you read—ask God to help you understand.
- Highlight what stands out to you.
- If you have questions, write them down!
- As you read, ask if there's something you can apply to your life today.

A Promise to Deposit

Salvation is a gift.

For by grace you have been saved through faith.
And this is not your own doing; it is the gift of
God, not a result of works, so that no one may
boast. For we are his workmanship, created in
Christ Jesus for good works, which God pre-
pared beforehand, that we should walk in them.

Ephesians 2:8–10

At its core, the gospel is offensive to the human mind and
will. Paul even goes a step further in 1 Corinthians 1:18:
"For the word of the cross is folly [foolishness!] to those
who are perishing, but to us who are being saved it is the
power of God."

Remember from last week that the simplest definition
of grace is undeserved favor. Ephesians 2 reveals this undeserved favor is not something you can work for. It's not
something you can boast about. It really has nothing to do
with *you* (v. 8)! This is so counterintuitive, but it's also what
makes Christianity unique among the world religions.

Every other religion entails some version of people
working their way to God (or gods), to enlightenment, or
to self-actualization through their self-efforts and merit.

Within these religions, people find salvation by working hard, doing good, and going through the motions of religious practices and habits. These efforts can result in two different outcomes: They can stoke our deep desire for self-glory, often providing the perfect breeding ground for pride to take root and flourish (or fester!). Or that same human effort can lead to a sense of hopelessness as we continually find ourselves in cycles of failure and shame.

But the gospel comes in and launches a full-on assault against humanity's own self-fabricated religious systems and strongholds. The gospel provokes by inviting you into the great paradox of God's design. You can see this in John 6:28–29: "Then they said to him [Jesus], 'What must we do, to be doing the works of God?' Jesus answered them, 'This is the work of God, that you *believe* in him whom he has sent.'"

God does the work while we bring nothing to the table. So what must we do? Believe.

Trust that Jesus is who he says he is and that he accomplished what Scripture says he did. (See Week 1.)

- So I can do nothing to merit God's favor? Correct.
- So there is no way to be righteous before God on my own and through my own self-efforts (Ecclesiastes 7:20)? Correct.
- Because of sin, even my righteousness is polluted before a holy God (Isaiah 64:6)? Correct.
- Yet God gives me salvation despite all that? Correct.

So what is there left to boast about? One answer: Jesus and *his* sacrifice for your sin in your place (Galatians 6:14).

Share with the one walking with you through this book about the greatest birthday or Christmas gift you ever received. What made the gift so significant? Also, when you receive an incredible gift, how does this shape your view of the gift-giver? How does it shape your thinking and affections toward the gift-giver? Here's the point: if God graciously saved you from your sins (past, present, and future) and gave you a new life, purpose, and an unshakable hope, how should this shape your affections toward such a good and merciful God? Take some time to pray now (out loud!) and thank God for the gift of salvation.

A Truth to Discover

Jesus is the source of your righteousness.

Wayne Grudem, in *Systematic Theology*, says this about the biblical concept of justification: "Justification is an instantaneous legal act of God in which he (1) thinks of our sins as forgiven and Christ's righteousness as belonging to us, and (2) declares us to be righteous in his sight."[2] As a follower of Jesus, you must grow in a right understanding of justification. It's been said that you can think of justification as "*Just as if* I had never sinned." This is a cute play on words, but it doesn't come close to capturing the power and reality of this scriptural truth.

The Christian's justification before God is astounding because we have sinned, and we still do! Yet because of our belief in the person and work of Jesus, God not only cancels the record of our sin debt but also transfers the righteousness of Jesus to our ledger. Keep in mind: this is not a transferal of *actual* righteousness according to Scripture.

Why is this important? For many who trust and follow Jesus:

> It can be a huge discouragement when
> they discover that upon becoming a
> Christian, their struggles and problems
> don't magically disappear.

Having a realistic expectation of Paul's meaning when he says you are now "in Christ" is important. Warren Wiersbe says it like this: "Though the penalty and the power of sin have been dealt with, the presence of sin still remains."[3]

Romans 4:3–5 says this:

> For what does the Scripture say? "Abraham believed God, and it was counted to him as righteousness." Now to the one who works, his wages are not counted as a gift but as his due. And to the one who does not work but believes in him who justifies the ungodly, his faith is counted as righteousness.

Ligonier Ministries provides this explanation of justification:

> When Paul develops the doctrine of justification by faith alone, he is saying that when God counts somebody righteous on the basis of faith, it is not because He looks at them and sees that they are inherently righteous. Rather, they have been clothed by the imputation, or transfer, of the righteousness of Christ to that person by faith.[4]

Read and discuss Romans 3:21–26. (Sidenote: "propiti-ation" is a big, fancy theological word that means "to appease the wrath of God" for sin.) Read and discuss Romans 10:9–10.

In their day-to-day life, people tend to be all over the place when it comes to their feelings and perception of their spiritual condition. Maybe right now you feel wonderful. Or maybe you feel like you're utterly failing! Perhaps today you especially feel the effects of persisting sin and the brokenness that accompanies it.

Pause and let this sink in:

Justification means that God sees your trust in Jesus, which means he now sees you through the lens of Jesus' righteousness.

Wow! That is why it was not only Jesus' death on the cross for sin that was significant. It was also his perfect life of righteousness and obedience.

So here's what you need to ask: If I am justified (made right with God and receive the righteousness of God) apart from my works, what role do my good works and righteousness now play?

Great question!

Paul helps us out in Ephesians 2:10: "For we are his workmanship, created in Christ Jesus for good works, which God prepared beforehand, that we should walk in them."

Here's the big idea: You are saved *for* good works, not *by* your good works. We see this interchange between faith and works in Titus 2:11–14:

> For the grace of God has appeared, bringing salvation for all people, training us to renounce ungodliness and worldly passions, and to live self-controlled, upright, and godly lives in the present age, waiting for our blessed hope, the appearing of the glory of our great God and Savior Jesus Christ, who gave himself for us to redeem us from all lawlessness and to purify for himself a people for his own possession who are zealous for good works.

Good works absolutely have their place in the Christian faith. Good works will absolutely flow from a life transformed by the good news that Jesus was crucified for sin and raised again. The whole purpose of the Christian life is about responding to the mercy and goodness of God in worship, and then subsequently pouring our lives out for the sake of others so they may know Jesus and follow him.

Discussion

1. Why is the "gift" of salvation so difficult for some to receive? Before you became a Christian, what were some barriers that kept you from embracing this gift?

_____

_____

_____

2. How are you doing with your expectations of the Christian life? Do you find yourself discouraged when sin still rears its ugly head? How does the doctrine of justification bring assurance and peace?

_____

_____

_____

_____

_____

3. Discuss some areas of pride in your own life and heart. Now read Galatians 6:14 and talk about the importance of "boasting" in Jesus and his death on the cross for you.

_____

_____

_____

_____

_____

4. Do you have questions about this truth to discover?

_____

_____

_____

_____

A Habit to Develop: Bible Reading

Read Psalm 119:11; 2 Timothy 3:16–17; Romans 10:17.
Discuss the importance of Bible reading.

God speaks primarily through the Bible (his Word). Continue utilizing the questions and pointers under the A Passage to Dive Into section. Here are some action points to consider as you read the Bible:

- Though many different approaches exist to reading the Bible, perhaps the primary two are inductive Bible study and reading the Bible as literature. Bible study entails breaking down Scripture one verse at a time and digging deep into each individual part. This is a fantastic way to read the Bible and grow in your understanding. Reading the Bible as literature is a better approach for reading large portions of the Bible (several chapters at a time). This is a great approach for getting a "big picture" understanding and for consistently reading through the entire Bible.
- Have a game plan for reading! Plan to continue reading the Bible after these eight weeks are up.
- A great goal for the Christian life is to read through the Bible each year.

Life in Christ

A Passage to Dive Into

Read Mark 11–16 this week.

We recommend reading a chapter each day (Monday–Friday). As you read, ask yourself the following questions:

1. What does this passage reveal about God?
2. What does it reveal about humanity/me?
3. Is there a command of God that I can obey? How can I apply this passage to my life this week? Is there any sin that I need to confess?
4. How does this passage point me to Jesus?

Pointers

- Don't get overwhelmed!
- Pray as you read—ask God to help you understand.
- Highlight what stands out to you.
- If you have questions, write them down!
- As you read, ask if there's something you can apply to your life today.

A Promise to Deposit

God has given you a whole new identity.
He is the author of the "jumpstart"!

Therefore, if anyone is in Christ, he
is a new creation. The old has passed
away; behold, the new has come.

2 Corinthians 5:17

Here you see that unique phrase again: "in Christ." This
points you back to the biblical truth of justification. (See
Week 2.) But this verse also takes you all the way back to
Genesis 1–2 and God's original design for creation. In the
beginning, before sin entered the world, Adam and Eve
experienced perfect harmony with God, with one another, and with creation. They experienced perfect peace and
wholeness. They also experienced an unfractured identity.

Merriam-Webster defines identity as "the distinguish-
ing character or personality of an individual or the relation
established by psychological identification."[5] Essentially,
Adam and Eve understood their source of life, significance,
and purpose flowed from God and from their relationship
with him. Everything proceeded from this primary identity of being an image bearer of God (Genesis 1:26–27)
and being in right relationship with the Creator. But after

sin entered God's perfect world, the disastrous effects on his creation were immediately felt. Sin distorted and fractured the identity of humanity. Now, people look for their primary identity in all the wrong places:

- Sexuality
- Work and achievements
- Physical appearance
- Family
- Creativity
- Community of people (sports team, organization, etc.)
- Being a good Christian
- Trauma
- Politics
- Ethnicity
- In _____

All these things encompass a *part* of who we are, but they are poor substitutes for a primary identity. And each eventually will buckle under the pressure of our expectations and hopes because none was designed to satisfy our hearts like God.

Where have you been tempted (and perhaps still are tempted) to find your primary identity? Like expecting water from a dried-up well, maybe you've experienced firsthand the emptiness of placing your identity in the wrong things. One of the incredible promises of Scripture is that when you trust and follow Jesus, God gives you a whole new identity. But the reality is that finding your identity in God was part of his plan from the beginning.

Moving forward in your new journey with Christ, life will continue to be messy at times. Remember, you're still in process, and though you live in a Google culture, you can't Google yourself to instant Christian maturity! However, over time, as you immerse yourself in the Bible and stay connected to a Christian community, you will begin taking these fractured pieces (see the above list!) and discovering their rightful place in relationship to who God is, what his Word says, and who he says *you* are.

Perhaps the defining biblical passage on Christian identity is Romans 6:1–14. Take some time to read through this passage.

Write down questions regarding anything you might not understand. What is your biggest takeaway from these verses? Share your questions and insights with the one walking with you through these eight weeks.

A Truth to Discover

The Christian life is living in response to redemption and in light of restoration.

Now we begin to get into some of the nuts and bolts of what it means to know and follow Jesus. Hopefully, you took the time to read Romans 6:1–14. (You may want to read it more than once!) A lot of "meat" is there, but here's what it says in simple terms: God's design is for you to live a life that is not dominated and decimated by sin. God desires that you live a life of freedom and purpose "in Christ." But don't think of freedom as "freedom to do what I want;" rather, think of freedom as "freedom to live for God in response to his mercy and no longer at the mercy of my sin."

Romans 6:6 may be offensive to some. After all, who wants to think of themselves as "enslaved" by sin? Remember, before God's intervention and rescue, our sin not only separated us from God but also bound us to a life of unbelief and rebellion against God. So much so that Romans 3:10–12 reveals that (apart from God) people not only persist in sin (unrighteousness) but also don't even seek after God! But praise God that "in Christ" he has not only worked redemption for you (setting you free from the penalty and power of sin) but also now works in you to restore his image within you. Essentially, God gave you a whole new life "in Christ" (Romans 6:11).

So much of the Christian journey entails believing what God has already accomplished for you as declared in the Bible.

For example, God has forgiven your sins (past, present, and future), and you don't have to fear condemnation (Romans 8:1). Presently, God sees you through the lens of Jesus' righteousness because of your trust in Jesus. Now your job is to respond by aligning your life with the life of Jesus and to reflect *his* righteousness to the world around you. This is what Paul talks about in Romans 6:13.

So what does that look like? First, it looks like a journey! There are no shortcuts. Ask the one walking with you through this process, and they'll tell you that their "life in Christ" has been a journey filled with ups and downs, defeats and victories, and everything in between. However, over time, the goal is to grow spiritually. The goal is to persevere in finding your primary identity "in Christ."

Also, it's not like you are living your life in a vacuum! Far from it, the pull of this world and of the culture will constantly tempt you to believe its lies—to pull you away from the Word of God and to push you to finding your identity in all the wrong places. This is why Colossians 3:1–3 says this:

> If then you have been raised with Christ, seek the things that are above, where Christ is, seated at the right hand of God. Set your minds on things that are above, not on things that are on earth. For you have died, and your life is hidden with Christ in God.

"Set your mind on things that are above" . . . this is easier said than done. Why? Because you are immersed in a world that is in rebellion against God. But hopefully a huge part of your believing and following Jesus stems from coming to the end of yourself while realizing the empty pursuits and promises of this world are just that: empty.

So moving forward, here's what you need to know: You are not who you were. You are not defined by your sin. You are not defined by the brokenness within or the brokenness of the world around you. You are a "new creation" (2 Corinthians 5:17). You are defined by who you are "in Christ."

In fact, Philippians 4:13 says this: "I can do all things through him who strengthens me." *All things.* That's a bold statement. In American culture, this verse is often taken out of context or used flippantly to say you can "hit that home run" or "get that promotion" through Christ. But in the context of Philippians, Paul says he can do all things through Christ even during extremely difficult circumstances (persecution, hardship, need).

That may be your situation. You may be walking through some hard things right now, and you're wondering:

- How do I navigate that relationship now that I'm following Jesus?
- How do I overcome this specific sin that for so long has gotten the best of me?
- How do I get through this financial difficulty?
- How do I cope with this loneliness and depression?
- How do I forgive that person who wronged and hurt me deeply?

Maybe you're walking through something else, and up until this point, you've attempted to navigate through it in your own strength. You've drawn from your own resources, thinking, and solutions. And you've run into one dead end after another.

Here's the good news: You've got this. You can do *all* things. But not in a "pull yourself up by the bootstraps" sort of way. You've got this because that old you is no more. God gave you a new identity in Jesus. As you focus on living your life through and for Jesus, he will strengthen and guide you through whatever life has in store.

Discussion

1. Read Ephesians 4:17–24 and discuss how your role as a new follower of Jesus is to "put on the new self" (Ephesians 4:24).

_____

_____

2. Memorize Galatians 2:20 and talk about the
   significance of this verse with the one walking with
   you through this eight-week process.

_____

_____

_____

_____

_____

3. Do you have questions about this truth to discover?

_____

_____

_____

_____

_____

A Habit to Develop: Prayer and Fasting

*Read Matthew 6:5–13 and 1 Thessalonians 5:17
to learn about prayer. Read Matthew 6:16–18
and Acts 13:2–3 to learn about fasting.*

Discuss the importance of prayer and fasting. Here are some action points to consider as you pray and fast:

- Prayer is simply a conversation with God.
- You don't have to use fancy theological words; you simply must recognize your need to be connected to God and hear his voice.
- Get into the habit of praying often *and* praying with your Bible open.
- Use Matthew 6:9–13 as a model for structuring your more focused times of prayer.
- Fasting heightens your desire for God—it fuels yearning for God *and* yearning to fight against the idols of your heart.
- Though the primary biblical form of fasting entails fasting from food, Christians can "fast" from social

media, technology, and other things as well to focus their attention on God.

- Fasting is especially helpful in times of decision-making and desperation.

Life in Community

A Passage to Dive Into

Read Galatians 1–6 this week.

We recommend reading a chapter each day (Monday–Friday). As you read, ask yourself the following questions:

1. What does this passage reveal about God?
2. What does it reveal about humanity/me?
3. Is there a command of God that I can obey? How can I apply this passage to my life this week? Is there any sin that I need to confess?
4. How does this passage point me to Jesus?

Pointers

- Don't get overwhelmed!
- Pray as you read—ask God to help you understand.
- Highlight what stands out to you.
- If you have questions, write them down!
- As you read, ask if there's something you can apply to your life today.

A Promise to Deposit

*God is a relational God who desires
a relationship with you.*

We learned in Week 1 that God demonstrated his love for a broken world by giving the gift of his Son, Jesus. This week we'll dive deeper into the reality of a relational God who pursues and makes promises to people. The big picture story (or the "metanarrative") of the Bible is the account of a relational God who redeems people.

In Genesis, we see God "walking" in the garden (Genesis 3:8) with Adam and Eve, calling out, "Where are you?" (Genesis 3:9). (Sidenote: God knew exactly where they were!) Even as Adam and Eve scrambled to conceal themselves from God, laden with guilt and shame, God sought them out. And though they experienced immediate consequences for their sin (Genesis 3:14–19), God's mercy was on display in both 1) a promise of future victory over Satan and sin (Genesis 3:15) and 2) the provision of a sacrificial substitute as God transferred his judgment for sin to an animal (Genesis 3:21).

From here, the rest of the Old Testament builds to the anticipation of a redemption that is to come. From Noah, to Abraham, to Isaac, Jacob, and Joseph, we see God's relational nature and his commitment to this promise of redemption. From Moses, to Joshua, through the time of the judges and into the kings, we continue to see God revealing himself to people, revealing more of himself and his ways. But through it all, we find this continual thread of redemptive activity. The prophets throughout the Old Testament (Elijah, Elisha, Isaiah, Jeremiah, Ezekiel, Hosea, Micah, and more) acted as God's mouthpiece to Israel to warn them when they were getting off-track. The prophets called out the people's idolatry, their injustice, and immorality. But even in this, we see God's gracious provision.

God doesn't owe anyone a warning! After all, he is perfect and holy, and his standard has never shifted or moved. Yet he patiently puts up with a creation in rebellion against him, his design, and dominion. As the Old Testament ends, we see the failure of Israel's kings to reflect the image of God. We see the failure of the people (Israel as a whole) to reflect his image, his heart, and his character. The world still waited in suspense for the fulfillment of this promise of redemption.

And then . . . Jesus.

> The true light, which gives light to everyone, was coming into the world. He was in the world, and the world was made through him, yet the world did not know him. He came to his own, and his own people did not receive him. But to all who did receive him, who believed in his name, he gave the right to become children of God, who were born, not of

blood nor of the will of the flesh nor of the will of man, but of God. And the Word became flesh and dwelt among us, and we have seen his glory, glory as of the only Son from the Father, full of grace and truth. (John 1:9–14, the "true light"/the "Word" was Jesus.)

In this the love of God was made manifest among us, that God sent his only Son into the world, so that we might live through him. In this is love, not that we have loved God but that he loved us and sent his Son to be the propitiation for our sins. (1 John 4:9–10, "propitiation" is the appeasement of God's holy wrath.)

Remember, Jesus *is* the image of the invisible God (Colossians 1:15). In John 14:9, Jesus said, "Whoever has seen me has seen the Father." Jesus is the culmination of God's pursuit of a relationship with humanity!

Do you want to know God? Have you ever thought: *If I just had a picture of God* . . . or, *If God would just reveal himself to me plainly* . . . guess what? He has! Jesus is the ultimate and final revelation of a relational God. Even as we come to the end of the Bible, we see the completion of God's plan

> Jesus is the ultimate and final revelation of a relational God.

from the beginning. We see the longing of a relational God fulfilled in *his* timing: "And I heard a loud voice from the throne saying, 'Behold, the dwelling place of God is with man. He will dwell with them, and they will be his people, and God himself will be with them as their God'" (Revelation 21:3).

So what does this mean for you as a new follower of Jesus? Sometimes you will be tempted to believe God has abandoned you or has withdrawn his presence from you. During those moments and seasons, you must cling to the promise of a relational God.

You must cling to the hope of a God who persists in pursuing you, still sees you, knows you, and loves you. Ultimately, the goal is to hold fast to your relationship with Jesus. Take time (right now!) to praise God for being a relational God who loves and pursues you!

_____

_____

_____

_____

_____

_____

_____

_____

_____

A Truth to Discover

God exists in a triune form.

Admittedly, there is much mystery in the biblical teaching of the Trinity. Christians have historically believed one God eternally exists in three persons: the Father, Son, and Holy Spirit. In this Trinity, God exists in perfect relationship within himself. The Father, Son, and Holy Spirit are co-existent, co-equal, and co-eternal. The Father is not the Son, and the Son is not the Holy Spirit (there *is* distinction), yet Christians affirm each as God in one individual being. Each has precisely the same nature, attributes, and perfections, and each is equally worthy of the same honor, faith, and obedience.

Over the years, some have attempted to explain the Trinity using the illustration of ice, water, and steam. Or another illustration often has been the egg with its outer shell, the egg white, followed by the yolk. Others have used a three-leaf clover to describe the biblical concept. Ultimately, each example breaks down and fails to capture fully the immense complexity and wonder of God existing in a triune form.

Even the early church needed a jumpstart to rightly understand God! The church (Christian leaders from all over the globe) gathered in councils 1,700 years ago

53

to combat destructive, false teachings and to formulate official church stances on important issues and doctrines. Though finalized in AD 451 at the Council of Chalcedon, the origins of the Nicene Creed can be traced back to the Council of Nicea in AD 325. This creed became especially foundational and formative for the church because it shaped how the church understood and worshiped a "triune God."

The Nicene Creed

We believe in one God, the Father almighty, maker of heaven and earth, of all things visible and invisible.

We believe in one Lord Jesus Christ, the only Son of God, begotten from the Father before all ages, God from God, Light from Light, true God from true God, begotten, not made; of the same essence as the Father. Through him all things were made. For us and for our salvation he came down from heaven; he became incarnate by the Holy Spirit and the virgin Mary, and was made human. He was crucified for us under Pontius Pilate; he suffered and was buried. The third day he rose again, according to the Scriptures. He ascended to heaven and is seated at the right hand of the Father. He will come again with glory to judge the living and the dead. His kingdom will never end.

And we believe in the Holy Spirit, the Lord, the giver of life. He proceeds from the Father and the Son, and with the Father and the Son is worshiped and glorified. He spoke through the prophets. We believe in one holy catholic [worldwide] and apostolic church. We affirm one baptism for the forgiveness of sins. We look forward to the resurrection of the dead, and to life in the world to come. Amen.

Important Trinitarian Passages

- "According to the foreknowledge of God the Father, in the sanctification of the Spirit, for obedience to Jesus Christ and for sprinkling with his blood: may grace and peace be multiplied to you" (1 Peter 1:2).

- "When the Spirit of truth comes, he will guide you into all the truth, for he will not speak on his own authority, but whatever he hears he will speak, and he will declare to you the things that are to come. He will glorify me (Jesus), for he will take what is mine and declare it to you. All that the Father has is mine; therefore I said that he will take what is mine and declare it to you" (John 16:13–15).

- "But when the goodness and loving kindness of God our Savior appeared, he saved us, not because of works done by us in righteousness, but according to his own mercy, by the washing of regeneration and renewal of the Holy Spirit, whom he poured

out on us richly through Jesus Christ our Savior"
(Titus 3:4–6).

- "But you, beloved, building yourselves up in your
  most holy faith and praying in the Holy Spirit, keep
  yourselves in the love of God, waiting for the mercy
  of our Lord Jesus Christ that leads to eternal life"
  (Jude 1:20–21).

- "How much more will the blood of Christ, who
  through the eternal Spirit offered himself without
  blemish to God, purify our conscience from dead
  works to serve the living God" (Hebrews 9:14).

- "And it is God who establishes us with you in Christ,
  and has anointed us, and who has also put his seal
  on us and given us his Spirit in our hearts as a
  guarantee" (2 Corinthians 1:21–22).

Okay, at this point, you may be thinking, *My brain
hurts trying to wrap my mind around this Trinity thing.*
Welcome to the club! Though the Scriptures clearly teach
God has revealed himself in triune form, it doesn't mean
we fully understand it! Maybe you're wondering, *Why is
this so important? After all, what does the Trinity have to do
with me?*

But think about it like this: If you are created in the
image of God, then God must be
relational. Why? Because from birth
to death, people are hardwired for
relationship! We need our mother
and father and family. We seek

People are
hardwired for
relationship!

56

friendship and companionship. We seek a partner in marriage, someone whom we can fully know and who can fully know us. People are built for community with one another. God built *you* for community and relationship. Though you might struggle to relate to a solitary God, you must strangely confess that a God self-existent in relationship within himself is more relatable!

Also, here's another crazy thought: it's not as though the Father, Son, and Holy Spirit were hanging out in eternity past bored out of their mind, playing ping pong, or trying to figure out how to pass the time. They didn't feel incomplete or lack something within the Trinity. No, there was (and is!) an eternally perfect love, joy, harmony, fellowship, and life within the Trinity. And out of the overflow of this *life*, the triune God decided to share his life with creation. Now that's pretty incredible.

A relational God . . . who exists in relationship . . . seeks a relationship with *you*! Praise God!

Discussion

1. Take some time to discuss with the person walking with you through these eight weeks how God has specifically sought and pursued a relationship with you.

57

_____

_____

2. Read back over the Trinitarian passages. Which ones are most significant to you? Why?

_____

_____

_____

_____

_____

3. Do you have any questions about this truth to discover?

_____

_____

_____

_____

_____

A Habit to Develop:
Biblical Community

Read Hebrews 10:24–25;
1 Corinthians 10:25–27; Acts 2:42–47. Discuss
the importance of biblical community.

Every Christian belongs to the worldwide church. They are all part of a global body of Christ. However, only in a local church community can a Christian know others and be fully known. In a local church community a Christian has personal accountability, a specific mission, a specific church leadership to submit to, and a place where they can regularly, actively use their specific gifts. Here are some action points to consider regarding biblical community:

- There is no such thing as a Lone Ranger Christian! The Bible describes the church as the body of Christ (1 Corinthians 12). *You* must get connected to a local church community, because as a follower of Jesus, you have been designed and hardwired for meaningful Christ-centered relationships.
- Following Jesus is hard. Unless you're in a context completely devoid of the gospel and any local church activity or influence, following Jesus *alone* is not God's will for you. Don't just make biblical

community "a" priority. Make it "the" priority as you continue to grow in your new faith. Find a local church that preaches and teaches the Bible. Find a local church that is devoted to making disciples of Jesus. Find a local church that calls you into a mission, not into consumership.

Life in the Spirit

A Passage to Dive Into

Read Ephesians 1-6 this week.

We recommend reading a chapter each day (Monday–Friday). As you read, ask yourself the following questions:

1. What does this passage reveal about God?
2. What does it reveal about humanity/me?
3. Is there a command of God that I can obey? How can I apply this passage to my life this week? Is there any sin that I need to confess?
4. How does this passage point me to Jesus?

Pointers

- Don't get overwhelmed!
- Pray as you read—ask God to help you understand.
- Highlight what stands out to you.
- If you have questions, write them down!
- As you read, ask if there's something you can apply to your life today.

A Promise to Deposit

Life is found in the Holy Spirit.

Hopefully, the past month has been a month of spiritual growth as you've been learning more of what it looks like to know and follow Jesus. We examined God's incredible love, his gifts of grace and salvation as well as what life "in Christ" and in community entails. At this point, you might be tempted to believe that moving forward, it's all on you, right? You might think, *Now I just need to dig in and work hard to get this Christianity thing down!*

In fact, the Bible teaches that the Holy Spirit is not only instrumental in drawing us to believe the gospel and trust in Jesus' righteousness, death, and resurrection, which results in our justification (Week 2), but also the Spirit is our power source for continued growth in our faith and in God's mission. The fancy theological word for this is "sanctification." The simplest definition of "sanctification" is "growth in likeness to Christ."

> "Sanctification" is "growth in likeness to Christ."

Unfortunately, if you don't have a solid handle on *who* the Holy Spirit is, you can easily misunderstand his role in your new life "in Christ." We've already seen that the Holy

Spirit *is* God. More specifically, he is the third member of the Trinity. Here's what the Holy Spirit is not:

- He is not some mystical force to be wielded and used (i.e., *Star Wars*!).
- He is not some magical genie at your beck and call (i.e., *Aladdin*!).
- He is not impersonal.
- He is not any *less* God than the Father or the Son!

Remember the Nicene Creed (Week 4)? It says, "We believe in the Holy Spirit, the Lord, the giver of life. He proceeds from the Father and the Son, and with the Father and the Son is worshiped and glorified."

Let's connect the dots. The Spirit of God is the "giver of life." You might think, *Wait a minute! I'm pretty sure my life came from my parents. (Shout out to Mom and Dad!) My life comes from the blood flowing through my veins right now. My life comes from the next breath that I'm about to draw.* True. Your physical life is bound up in all those things. But in John 3:1–15, Jesus had an interesting conversation with a religious leader named Nicodemus. He essentially told Nicodemus that he needed to be born again! Of course, Nicodemus was baffled and confused. At one point, in John 3:5, Jesus said, "Truly, truly, I say to you, unless one is born of water and the Spirit, he cannot enter the kingdom of God."

In Week 3, we talked about how God has given you a whole new identity "in Christ" (an identity that was fractured and lost back in Genesis 3). But this new identity can only be accessed through the transformative work of the Holy Spirit. Only the Holy Spirit can connect you to your new life in Christ. Much like a car without a battery, there is no jumpstarting the discipleship process without the Holy Spirit. The apostle John said in John 6:63: "It is the Spirit who gives life; the flesh is no help at all. The words that I have spoken to you are spirit and life." In fact: Without the empowering presence of the Holy Spirit, it is *impossible* for you to live from your new identity "in Christ."

Conversely, someone who has not trusted Jesus can only live from one identity and nature: the old nature that is still bent toward unbelief and rebellion against God. A Christian on the other hand (that's you!) has a whole new identity from which to draw! However, this is only accomplished through the work of the Holy Spirit within you.

Check out the apostle Paul's take in Romans 8:2–6:

> For the law of the Spirit of life has set you free in Christ Jesus from the law of sin and death. For God has done what the law, weakened by the flesh, could not do. By sending his own Son in the likeness of sinful flesh and for sin, he condemned sin in the flesh, in order that the righteous requirement of the law might be fulfilled in us, who walk not according to the flesh but according to the Spirit. For those who live according to the flesh set their minds on the things of the flesh, but those who live according to

the Spirit set their minds on the things of the Spirit. For to set the mind on the flesh is death, but to set the mind on the Spirit is life and peace.

Now, one caveat: in the New Testament, the biblical concept of flesh is found in the Greek word *sarx*. Don't think of "flesh" in terms of your "skin flesh." Though it absolutely can mean "the material that covers the bones of a human body or animal," Paul often used *sarx* to describe the human condition. More specifically, it came to be synonymous with the fallenness/sinfulness of humanity apart from God. Understanding this is important, especially when reading a passage like Romans 8!

So what does all this mean for you?

For starters, it means God gave you an Advocate (himself). More on that later! It's not solely on *you* to work out your sanctification ("growth in likeness to Christ"). This is incredibly encouraging!

Why? Because at times you might feel like you're not growing. You might feel like you're going backward. You're going to continue to struggle with the presence of sin in your life. But remember, the Holy Spirit connects you to your new identity "in Christ" that God has promised.

Praise God! You're not the "old you." Your identity has changed. Your thoughts, affections, and purpose have all changed. Your *life* has changed! Moving forward, you must understand that your new *life* is found in the Holy Spirit.

A Truth to Discover

*The Holy Spirit is God as well as God's
gift for your Christian growth.*

Considering how many have sought to malign and misuse the Holy Spirit, a new Christ follower must have a clear picture of not only *who* he is but also *what* he does. The apostle John referred to the Holy Spirit as "the Helper," which comes from the Greek word *parakletos*. Let's break that down: *para* means "alongside" and *kletos* means "to call." So *parakletos* is someone called to stand alongside another. Though "Helper" only scratches the surface of the significance of this word, it's a good start. But as a follower of Jesus, how does the Holy Spirit "come alongside" *you*?

Perhaps some of the most powerful chapters in all of Scripture illuminating the role of the Holy Spirit come in John 14–16. When you have time, you should read through these chapters in their entirety! For now, here is what the apostle John had to say about the Holy Spirit:

- "And I will ask the Father, and he will give you another Helper, to be with you forever, even the Spirit of truth, whom the world cannot receive, because it neither sees him nor knows him. You

know him, for he dwells with you and will be in you"
(John 14:16–17).

- "But the Helper, the Holy Spirit, whom the Father
will send in my name, he will teach you all things
and bring to your remembrance all that I have said to
you" (John 14:26).

- "But when the Helper comes, whom I will send
to you from the Father, the Spirit of truth, who
proceeds from the Father, he will bear witness about
me. And you also will bear witness, because you have
been with me from the beginning" (John 15:26–27).

- "Nevertheless, I tell you the truth: it is to your
advantage that I go away, for if I do not go away,
the Helper will not come to you. But if I go, I
will send him to you. And when he comes, he will
convict the world concerning sin and righteousness
and judgment: concerning sin, because they do not
believe in me; concerning righteousness, because
I go to the Father, and you will see me no longer;
concerning judgment, because the ruler of this world
is judged" (John 16:7–11).

- "When the Spirit of truth comes, he will guide you
into all the truth, for he will not speak on his own
authority, but whatever he hears he will speak, and
he will declare to you the things that are to come.
He will glorify me, for he will take what is mine and
declare it to you. All that the Father has is mine;
therefore I said that he will take what is mine and
declare it to you" (John 16:13–15).

Just from these few passages, we can glean some important biblical truths of the functions of the Holy Spirit:

- Guides you in truth.
- Not only dwells with you but also within you.
- Dwells within you forever.
- Helps you recall/remember the teachings of Jesus.
- Bears witness about Jesus—who Jesus is, and what he has done.
- Empowers *your* witness to others (see Acts 1:8).
- Brings conviction of sin and your need for the righteousness of Jesus.
- Reveals things to come (at times).
- *Always* brings glory to Jesus.

In addition to these truths from John's Gospel, the Spirit plays a vital role in other areas as well:

- "Seals" you (Ephesians 1:13–14). More on this next week!
- "Regenerates" you (Titus 3:5–6). He gives you new life!
- Intercedes for you in your weakness and groaning (Romans 8:26–27).
- Produces "spiritual fruit" in your life that conforms your character to the character of Jesus (Galatians 5:22–23).

- Brings more *freedom* to your life!
  (2 Corinthians 3:17).
- Brings joy (1 Thessalonians 1:6).
- Helps you experience the outpouring of God's love
  (Romans 5:5).
- Helps you abound in hopefulness (Romans 15:13).
- Fills you (Ephesians 5:18) and leads you
  (Romans 8:14).
- Gives you victory over sinful desires (Galatians 5:16).
- Appoints you for specific missions (Acts 13:2).
- Anoints you with certain spiritual gifts
  (Romans 12:3–8; 1 Corinthians 12:1–11).
- Baptizes you (immerses you) into the body of Christ,
  the church (1 Corinthians 12:12–13).
- Unifies you with other Christians (Act 4:32).

At this point, you might need to pause because it might be overwhelming to see this (not even exhaustive) list. You might think: *Last week I just learned about this whole Trinity thing, and now you're telling me the Holy Spirit does all these things in my life?* He does! But . . . it's important to keep your focus on the main thing.

In his book *Who Is the Holy Spirit?*, while talking about the significance of why "Holy" is attached to the name of the third person of the Trinity, R. C. Sproul says:

> The term holy is attached to his title because of the particular task the Spirit performs in our redemption. Among the persons of the Trinity, the Spirit is the

principal actor who works for our sanctification ["growth in likeness to Christ"], enabling the process by which we are conformed to the image of Christ and made holy.[6]

What's the main thing? The Holy Spirit makes your life look more like Jesus. And that makes perfect sense if he's your only lifeline to your new identity "in Christ." Over time, as you allow the Holy Spirit to lead and guide, and as you surrender your will to him, your life will reflect the life of your Savior and Lord.

Finally, how do you know if an inclination, a prompting, or a feeling is originating from some other source, "spirit," or even from your own selfish desires? You "test" the spirit by evaluating it against the standard of the Holy Spirit's own truth as revealed in the Bible. Here's the simplest way to put it: the Holy Spirit (the Spirit of God) will *never* contradict the Word of God.

Discussion

1. Prior to becoming a Christian, did you have any misconceptions about the Holy Spirit? Also, think about a few special people in your life who have advocated for you and helped you. What does it mean that God is willing to come alongside you as your Advocate?

_____

_____

2. Take some time to read back through some of the roles
   of the Holy Spirit with the person walking with you
   through this book. Pick out two or three that stand
   out and share why they are significant to you.

_____

_____

_____

_____

_____

3. Do you have any questions about Romans 8:2–6? Do
   you have any questions about this truth to discover?

_____

_____

_____

_____

_____

A Habit to Develop: Confession

Read 1 John 1:9; James 5:16; Psalm 51. Discuss the importance of Christian confession.

Here are some action points to consider as you develop the habit of confession:

- There is *power* in confessing your sins (specifically) to God and to other Christians. As a follower of Jesus, you don't confess sins to become "saved" again. Rather, you confess sins to restore broken fellowship with God.
- God is all-knowing, so remember that you're not telling God anything he doesn't already know! However, confession is far more about allowing *your* heart to be broken over any sin in your life, and then going before God in prayer to agree with him that it is what it is— sinful.
- You know you are growing in spiritual maturity as a follower of Jesus when the time between your sin and the time between confession is shrinking.
- Ultimately, the biblical concept of the "fear of the Lord" entails a hatred of what is sinful in your life. It is getting to a place of despising the sin in your life and heart because you have a clear understanding

73

that this exact sin is why Christ had to die on
the cross.

- Take some time right now to confess to God some of
  the sinful areas of your heart that you've kept hidden.
- Read back over 1 John 1:9 and Romans 8:1, and then
  praise God for his grace and forgiveness!

Firm Foundation

A Passage to Dive Into

Read Philippians 1–4 this week.

We recommend reading a chapter each day (Monday–Thursday; on Friday, review and pray through what stood out to you the most from Philippians). As you read, ask yourself the following questions:

1. What does this passage reveal about God?
2. What does it reveal about humanity/me?
3. Is there a command of God that I can obey? How can I apply this passage to my life this week? Is there any sin that I need to confess?
4. How does this passage point me to Jesus?

Pointers

- Don't get overwhelmed!
- Pray as you read—ask God to help you understand.
- Highlight what stands out to you.
- If you have questions, write them down!
- As you read, ask if there's something you can apply to your life today.

A Promise to Deposit

God will never let you go.

This promise is *built* upon the truth of the previous weeks of spiritual discovery. Over the last several weeks, you've learned that God loves you with an unwavering, unconditional love that is rooted in his perfect character. His love is not dependent upon your performance. Far from it—even when you could not do anything to merit salvation, God generously supplied you with undeserved favor ("grace"). He alone is the source of your wisdom, righteousness, sanctification, and redemption (1 Corinthians 1:30). He is the source of spiritual and abundant life for the follower of Jesus.

Here's the great temptation at every turn for the Christian: As you grow in your faith, you will be tempted to revert to thinking that it's now "all on me." You'll be pulled back to self-reliance. When this happens, you may be overwhelmed with thoughts and feelings of fear and failure when you struggle and fall. Know that the Bible teaches that Satan is very real. Not only is Satan's role to "steal and kill and destroy" (John 10:10) but he also does not rest seeking to accuse followers of Jesus for their shortcomings and failures (Revelation 12:10). The apostle Peter tells us that Satan is like a "roaring lion, seeking someone to devour" (1 Peter 5:8). Why is this important to understand? Because the onslaught of Satan's attacks combined with your ongoing battle(s) with the "presence of sin" (Week 2) might lead you to doubt God's promises and faithfulness.

It's in these times that you need this reminder that God is faithful. He will never let you go. Take some time to read through John 10 in its entirety. Specifically, take some time to ponder the significance of these verses:

- "The thief comes only to steal and kill and destroy. I came that they may have life and have it abundantly. I am the good shepherd. The good shepherd lays down his life for the sheep" (John 10:10–11).
- "I am the good shepherd. I know my own and my own know me, just as the Father knows me and I know the Father; and I lay down my life for the sheep" (John 10:14–15).
- "My sheep hear my voice, and I know them, and they follow me. I give them eternal life, and they will never perish, and no one will snatch them out of my hand. My Father, who has given them to me, is greater than all, and no one is able to snatch them out of the Father's hand. I and the Father are one" (John 10:27–30).

Let these biblical promises of John 10:28–29 wash over you: You have eternal life. You will never perish. *No one* can snatch you away from God's hand.

Anyone can say that. Plenty of parents might tell their young child, "I'll protect you." Or, "Dad will always be there for you." Or perhaps, "Mom will never let you go." But here is the reality: we can't ultimately back up that promise! Why? Because we're fallible. We're limited. We don't know what the next day holds, let alone the next moment. As much as we don't want to admit it, we are powerless at times to safeguard ourselves or the ones we love. Forces greater than us are at work.

But John 10:29 reminds us that God "is greater than all." The God who is sovereign over all cannot and will not allow anyone or anything to rip you away from a relationship with him. No one can nullify his salvation or favor.

Your foundation "in Christ" is firm
because it's not built on your power
or ability alone to stay faithful.

It's built on the faithfulness of God. Praise God!

In a culture that desperately desires consistency, permanency, and faithfulness, we must collectively confess that we all fail to measure up. Even the best parents fail. Great leaders, politicians, presidents, and CEOs will disappoint. Stories abound of people being devastated when even pastors let them down. In the Old Testament, Israel's priests were ultimately flawed men trying to keep the righteous requirements of God before his people. Their priesthood was limited. Their offerings of sacrifices for sins were limited. But their ultimate purpose was to point ahead to Jesus.

This is what the author of Hebrews tells us:

> The former priests were many in number, because they were prevented by death from continuing in office, but he (Jesus) holds his priesthood permanently, because he continues forever. Consequently, he is able to save to the uttermost those who draw near to God through him, since he always lives to make intercession for them. (Hebrews 7:23–25)

Don't gloss over that. Jesus *lives* to make intercession for you.

Let's break it down like this: On your *worst* day, Jesus is still in heaven, acting as your intermediary (in your place). On your *worst* day, Jesus is your righteousness. On your *worst* day, God's forgiveness still holds. On your *worst* day, you can still draw near to God, and Jesus will not abandon you. He will not let you go.

Spend some time in prayer thanking God for the firm foundation you have "in Christ." Take some time to worship the one who will never leave you nor forsake you (Deuteronomy 31:6)!

_____

_____

_____

_____

A Truth to Discover

Every Christ follower is secure "in Christ."

First, let's clarify what it is meant by "the security of the Christian." Despite the rhetoric of many "prosperity and wealth" false teachers in some Christian circles, here is what is *not* meant:

- Security has nothing to do with God owing you money and material possessions.
- Security has nothing to do with God owing you good health.
- Security has nothing to do with God never allowing any physical harm or hardship to come your way.
- Security has nothing to do with God protecting you from relational adversity.
- Security has nothing to do with God protecting you from your own poor decisions!

Hopefully, you get the point. Remember, God is not *primarily* after your temporal happiness that can often be rooted in the things of this world. Instead, he's after your holiness! He's after your sanctification (Week 5). He wants your life to progressively look more and more like Jesus, knowing that one day your faith will become sight.

Colossians 3:4 tells us: "When Christ who is your life, appears, then you also will appear with him in glory." So let's continue to put the pieces together. This week in your Bible reading, hopefully you paused on Philippians 1:6, which says: "And I am sure of this, that he who began a good work in you will bring it to completion at the day of Jesus Christ."

Now, based on this verse, take a moment to quickly answer two questions:

- Who started the work of salvation in you?
- Who will finish that work? When? (Okay, that's a third question!)

Christian, God is thinking about something you're not thinking about. Yes, he knows you have that work deadline. Of course, he sees that frayed relationship. Yes, God knows your financial needs. Yes, he cares when you're hurting, sick, or . . . even dying. But God is already thinking about "the day of Christ Jesus" when you will come face to face with your Savior, Jesus. Even Jesus said this in John 6:37–40:

> All that the Father gives me will come to me, and whoever comes to me I will never cast out. For I have come down from heaven, not to do my own will but the will of him who sent me. And this is the will of him who sent me, that I should lose nothing of all that he has given me, but raise it up on the last day.

> For this is the will of my Father, that everyone who looks on the Son and believes in him should have eternal life, and I will raise him up on the last day.

The security of the Christian has everything to do with a faithful God who finishes what he starts.

Your security as a Christian (that's you!) means the God who connected you to your new life "in Christ" will persevere in his work in you until Christ returns or until you breathe your last and ascend to heaven where Jesus has prepared a place for you (John 14:1–3).

So when does this security kick in? Do you have to be a Christian for a certain amount of time? Do you need to earn your Christian merit badge? No! Remember, your foundation "in Christ" is firm because it's not built on your power or ability alone to stay faithful. It's built on the faithfulness of God. In fact, Paul reminds Christians of an important truth in Ephesians 1:13–14:

> And you also were included in Christ when you heard the message of truth, the gospel of your salvation. When you believed, you were marked in him with a seal, the promised Holy Spirit, who is a deposit guaranteeing our inheritance until the

> redemption of those who are God's possession—to
> the praise of his glory.

In ancient times, a king sealed an important letter or document with the "king's seal" and sent it with a courier to its intended destination. It was common knowledge that if the letter were opened or tampered with before it reached its intended target, the courier would have to answer to the king. No one was to break the king's seal.

Think of it like this: anyone with decent credit or means can put a deposit or a down payment on a home. They may have a great job. They may make plenty of money, but *nothing* is guaranteed. People lose their jobs. Unforeseen circumstances and hardships arise. No one can absolutely say they will follow through on their deposit. But God's deposit is always a good deposit. For example, 2 Corinthians 5:5 says, "He who has prepared us for this very thing is God, who has given us the Spirit as a guarantee."

Now, go back to Ephesians 1:13–14. When did God seal you with his Spirit? When did he make the deposit? At the moment you heard the gospel . . . and believed! Wow! *That* is why we say "in Christ" you have a firm foundation. You have an unshakable security.

But that doesn't mean you're absolved of human responsibility! The New Testament abounds with commands for the follower of Jesus to obey. This is why the apostle Paul says this in Philippians 2:12–13:

> Therefore, my beloved, as you have always obeyed, so now, not only as in my presence but much more in my absence, work out your own salvation with fear and trembling, for it is God who works in you, both to will and to work for his good pleasure.

For the rest of your life, you will "work out" your salvation, seeking to know God through his Word and grow in obedience to his commands. You will have to "work out" what it looks like to grow in grace, to grow in purity and patience, and to grow in honoring God with your speech, thoughts, habits, attitudes, and relationships.

But you will *never* have to work "for" your salvation because your ultimate confidence lies in Philippians 2:13: God through Jesus has already done the most important work in you! Let this truth sink in and give you confidence, not in yourself, but in the faithful God whose promises are true and who has never defaulted on a down payment!

Discussion

1. Have you ever wrestled with trust issues or a sense of abandonment due to others letting you down? How can you keep from projecting these previous experiences and expectations onto God?

2. In many parts of the country, foundation issues with homes are not a matter of "if" but "when"! Think about a beautiful, ornate three-story home with all the modern updates and amenities. Now imagine that same home built upon a cracked and crumbling foundation. The appearance of the house doesn't matter if the foundation is not firm. How can knowing that God is for you and that you are "secure in Christ" become the bedrock upon which to build your new Christian life?

_____

_____

_____

_____

_____

3. Do you have any questions about John 10? Do you have any questions about this truth to discover?

_____

_____

_____

_____

_____

A Habit to Develop: Worship

Read John 4:23–24; Romans 12:1–2; Psalm 95:1–3;
Revelation 7:9–10. Discuss the importance of
Christian worship.

Worship is first and foremost about what you value. In worship, God draws near as you draw near to him (James 4:8). Perhaps this is because when you worship God, you rightly respond to who he is, to what he has done, and to his character and ways. God reveals himself through worship because in worship we humble ourselves while exalting *him*. Warren Wiersbe says this: "Worship is the believer's response to all they are—mind, emotions, will, body—to what God is and says and does."[7]

Elsewhere, D. A. Carson describes worship like this:

> To worship God "in spirit and in truth" is first
> and foremost a way of saying that we must worship
> God by means of Christ. In him the reality has
> dawned, and the shadows are being swept away
> (Hebrews 8:13). Christian worship is new covenant
> worship; it is gospel-inspired worship; it is Christ-
> centered worship; it is cross-focused worship.[8]

Here are some action points to consider as you worship:

- Worship is about what you *treasure*. If you treasure God, you will praise him. You will surrender your will and life to him. You will cry out to him. It's less about the posture of your body (kneeling, standing, lying prostrate, etc.) and so much more about the posture of your heart. When you treasure Jesus, all of life becomes a continuous response of glorifying Jesus for who he is and what he has accomplished for you.

- In the Old Testament (specifically in the Psalms but in numerous other places as well), worship is primarily public and vocal. In the New Testament, the writers refer to both public and private worship. Today, we worship both ways: corporately with other Christ followers and privately to cultivate our personal devotion for Jesus.

- Some people worship best in quiet and solitude, others in community. Some prefer music. Some prefer to be outdoors in creation. The Bible has many examples of different forms of worship. Find out what forms and expressions work best for you to connect your heart to Jesus . . . and make worship a lifestyle!

Ultimate Authority

A Passage to Dive Into

Read Colossians 1–4 this week.

We recommend reading a chapter each day (Monday–Thursday; on Friday, review and pray through what stood out to you the most from Colossians). As you read, ask yourself the following questions:

1. What does this passage reveal about God?
2. What does it reveal about humanity/me?
3. Is there a command of God that I can obey? How can I apply this passage to my life this week? Is there any sin that I need to confess?
4. How does this passage point me to Jesus?

Pointers

- Don't get overwhelmed!
- Pray as you read—ask God to help you understand.
- Highlight what stands out to you.
- If you have questions, write them down!
- As you read, ask if there's something you can apply to your life today.

A Promise to Deposit

God is sovereign over all things.

Hopefully at this point, you've realized that one of the chief aims of this discipleship tool has been to build upon each of the previous weeks' promises and truths. Part of the reason we are talking about the sovereignty of God in Week 7 is simply this: once you embrace God as loving, gracious, relational, life-giving, and promise-keeping, then trusting and resting in his sovereignty isn't a tall task. But what do we mean by "sovereignty"?

Merriam-Webster defines sovereignty like this: "sovereignty: (a) supreme power especially over a body politic, (b) freedom from external control: (c) controlling influence."[9]

> When we talk about "God's sovereignty," we refer to his supreme right to do all things according to his standard and satisfaction.

Now if we were talking about a flawed and failure-prone "human sovereign," we might balk at giving our nod of approval to this much unchecked power. But here are a couple of questions to ponder:

1. What if that sovereign was *perfect*? And what if that sovereign was perfectly omniscient (all-knowing), omnipotent (all-powerful), and good?
2. What if, as instruments of his creation, we didn't get a "vote" or a "voice" in the scope of his sovereignty? What if he, simply by design and default, was already sovereign over all creation, regardless of how we *felt* about it?

Take a moment to soak up these promises written by Jeremiah and Isaiah, two Old Testament prophets. First, Jeremiah gave us the assurance that nothing is beyond the scope of God's sovereign power:

> Ah, Lord GOD! It is you who have made the heavens and the earth by your great power and by your outstretched arm! Nothing is too hard for you. (Jeremiah 32:17)

Then, Isaiah gave us a reminder of where we are headed and God's definitive role in getting us there:

> He will swallow up death forever; and the Lord GOD will wipe away tears from all faces, and the reproach of his people he will take away from all the earth, for the LORD has spoken. It will be said on that day, "Behold, this is our God; we have waited for him, that he might save us. This is the LORD; we have waited for him; let us be glad and rejoice in his salvation." (Isaiah 25:8–9)

Wow! Keep this future picture in mind. God has brought you to the place you are now. You are "in Christ," and one day God will complete what he started (Philippians 1:6). One day death will be no more. The brokenness, sadness, and the weight of our sins will be removed. And on that day, we will collectively recognize and celebrate that this restoration was accomplished by a sovereign God. In fact, throughout Scripture you'll find this undercurrent of God's sovereignty over all creation.

Notice in Genesis 1 a couple of recurring themes: As God created the world, the text repeatedly reminds us that "it was so" (Genesis 1:7, 9, 11, 15, 24, 30). "It was so" . . . because creation's only response to the voice of God is to submit to his sovereignty!

Another theme we see is that God declared his work as "good" (Genesis 1:4, 10, 12, 18, 21, 25, 31). This is immensely important! Why? Because in a culture of relativism, *many* things are labeled as "good" today. However, only a sovereign God can ultimately decide and dictate what is "good." He sets the standard because he *is* the standard! We'll circle back to this later!

God is sovereign over all things. Let that statement sit for a minute. This is a promise that must be accompanied by your ownership. Why?

- Because when life at times seems spiraling out of control . . .
- When the trials and tensions are overwhelming . . .

- When you are tempted to be jaded by the brokenness and darkness of the world . . .
- When you are enticed to place ultimate hope in human leaders and solutions . . .
- When you are engulfed by feelings of inadequacy or misled to trust in your own self-sufficiency . . .

God is sovereign over all things, and he is good. He is the ultimate and supreme good. You can trust that, even amid the brokenness and sin all around you, God moves and acts for his glory and your good.

A Truth to Discover

God is the ultimate authority over his creation.

God's authority flows from his sovereignty. What is the first thought that pops into your mind when you hear the word "authority"? For some, the word might recall a policeman or a politician. On the other hand, you might think of a boss, a judge, or even your parents. When we start talking about "authority," the problem is we don't have a perfect picture of human authority. So inevitably, we tend to veer to negative examples, and our concepts of authority are tainted with our flawed perception and pictures. In fact, our natural inclination (and the disposition of our heart!) is to push back against authority. This is no coincidence.

Read Isaiah 14:12–14. Though the early verses of Isaiah 14 seem to be directed at the king of Babylon, most Bible interpreters believe that a shift occurs in verse twelve, and the real instigator of rebellion is revealed. Satan despised the authority of God and sought to "make himself like the Most High" (v. 14). We can only speculate why Satan (as a created angel of God) was not content with the Creator/creation distinction, and now we see and feel the ripple effects of his rebellion. This DNA of resisting God's authority has been infused into the world, and we *all* feel the pull of wanting to believe we too should be "like the Most High."

But there is only one who can handle the burden of ultimate authority. Colossians 1:16–17 tells us: "For by him all things were created, in heaven and on earth, visible and invisible, whether thrones or dominions or rulers or authorities—all things were created through him and for him. And he is before all things, and in him all things hold together."

By way of reminder, Paul, the author of Colossians, is talking about Jesus here! In fact, Jesus said the same in Matthew 28:18: "All authority in heaven and on earth has been given to me."

And now we come back full circle to an important truth about authority. If Jesus (God in human flesh) is *the* standard of truth, righteousness, and justice, he alone is qualified and capable of setting the standard for all of creation.

A big part of the battle of the Christian life entails embracing the authority of Jesus over every square inch of your life . . . as well as his authority over all things!

In fact, significant spiritual growth cannot take place until this surrender to God's ultimate authority takes place.

God has authority over individuals and kingdoms. Throughout the Old Testament, we see God's authority over the lives of individuals (Adam, Noah, Abraham, Isaac, Jacob, Joseph, Moses, Joshua, Samuel, David, etc.). But it's important to comprehend that the scope of his authority also extends to nations and kingdoms as well. Far from the tenets of deism (that God set the world into motion but is now distant and detached from his creation), the Bible reveals that God orchestrates the rise and fall of nations, kingdoms, and kings all for his purposes and glory.

- "Know that the Most High rules the kingdom of men and gives it to whom he will. . . . All the inhabitants of the earth are accounted as nothing, and he does according to his will among the host of heaven and among the inhabitants of the earth; and none can stay his hand or say to him, 'What have you done?'" (Daniel 4:25, 35).

- "And he [God] made from one man every nation of mankind to live on all the face of the earth, having determined allotted periods and the boundaries of their dwelling place" (Acts 17:26).

- "For there is no authority except from God, and those that exist have been instituted by God" (Romans 13:1).

As you read through the Old Testament, particularly the prophetic books of Isaiah, Jeremiah, Ezekiel, and Daniel, it is hard to miss the absolute sovereign authority of

God over sinful nations and kingdoms to accomplish his divine will.

God has authority over the hearts and thoughts of people. Scripture reveals that humanity, created in the very image of God, has the free will to speak, think, act, and decide. However, humanity's freedom is always subject to the sovereign authority and will of God.

Here are a few examples:

- "The plans of the heart belong to man, but the answer of the tongue is from the LORD" (Proverbs 16:1).
- "Many are the plans in the mind of a man, but it is the purpose of the LORD that will stand" (Proverbs 19:21).
- "O LORD, you have searched me and known me! You know when I sit down and when I rise up; you discern my thoughts from afar. You search out my path and my lying down and are acquainted with all my ways. Even before a word is on my tongue, behold, O LORD, you know it altogether" (Psalm 139:1–4).

God has authority over salvation. Time does not permit us to revisit every instance of God's sovereign authority in the Bible. Suffice it to say, those who follow Jesus must come to an agreement on this point: we are *not* sovereign! Though many struggle trying to live under the illusion and facade of self-sovereignty, the reality is we are finite, limited, broken beings.

We don't even have authority over our next breath because we never fully know what the next moment holds (James 4:14–15). Though an element of mystery surrounds the biblical teaching of God's authority in salvation, the Bible undoubtedly teaches that prior to salvation we were "dead" in our sins (Ephesians 2:1–3), incapable of seeking him or practicing righteousness (Romans 3:10–12). Without God's loving intervention, we were without hope (Ephesians 2:12). We needed a sovereign God to intercede!

> Blessed be the God and Father of our Lord Jesus Christ, who has blessed us in Christ with every spiritual blessing in the heavenly places, even as he chose us in him before the foundation of the world, that we should be holy and blameless before him. In love he predestined us for adoption to himself as sons through Jesus Christ, according to the purpose of his will, to the praise of his glorious grace, with which he has blessed us in the Beloved. (Ephesians 1:3–6)

> And we know that for those who love God all things work together for good, for those who are called according to his purpose. For those whom he foreknew he also predestined to be conformed to the image of his Son, in order that he might be the firstborn among many brothers. And those whom he predestined he also called, and those whom he called

he also justified, and those whom he justified he also glorified. (Romans 8:28–30)

Let the significance of these verses sink in. God did not owe us his mercy or salvation. He was not obligated to rescue us from our unbelieving, rebellious state. Yet he stepped in and graciously called many to himself, while others he allowed to persist in their rebellion.

And though we might wrestle with the tension of where man's free will and God's sovereign authority collide, we must cling to the biblical promises that he is a perfect, righteous, and just authority. Following the lead of creation in Genesis 1, we submit to the Sovereign and trust that his plan is "good"!

R. C. Sproul states:

> Human freedom and divine sovereignty exist in a complex, mysterious relationship. Though God ordains all of our choices—even choices that end up being thwarted because they do not match the results that He has ordained—we can never blame Him for our sin. Neither can we escape responsibility for our actions. We have misunderstood Scripture if we think our choices are the final determiner of the course of our lives, but we have also misunderstood it if we deny human freedom.[10]

So what do you do with this truth? Paul in 1 Corinthians 8:6 tells us: "Yet for us there is one God, the Father, from whom are all things and for whom we exist, and one Lord, Jesus Christ, through whom are all things and through whom we exist."

The truth is you exist for God. If you will not only recognize but revere (esteem, worship) his ultimate authority, God will freely work in and through you to accomplish incredible work for the sake of the gospel and for your good.

Discussion

1. In your life, what has "authority" looked like?
   Reflect on your relationships with your parents, with previous bosses, or even your perception of leaders and authority figures. How have these human authorities shaped your view of God's sovereign authority over all things? Have you ever struggled to trust in God's goodness? After seven weeks of walking through the Bible, has your confidence in his goodness grown? In what way?

---

2. Reread Jesus' statement in Matthew 28:18. Are you holding anything back from his authority right now? Is there any area of your life where he does not have authority (e.g., your thinking, speech, relationships, habits)? Take some time to pray and confess where you may need to surrender to the *good* sovereign authority of your Savior.

_____

_____

_____

_____

_____

3. As you think about the different areas of God's authority and the accompanying Bible verses, do you have any questions? Do you have any questions about this truth to discover?

_____

_____

_____

_____

_____

A Habit to Develop: Giving

*Read Proverbs 3:9; 2 Corinthians 9:6–8;
Galatians 6:6–10; Matthew 6:19–21. Discuss
the importance of Christian giving.*

Giving flows from understanding the sovereign authority of God over all creation. If God has ultimate authority and ownership, the Christian's response must be to understand a key truth. We are *not* owners but stewards. Stewardship entails viewing yourself as a manager of the gifts and resources with which God entrusts you. And if your goal is to follow Jesus and to make disciples of Jesus (Matthew 28:19–20), then you must leverage your life, finances, talents, and "stuff" for the sake of the gospel.

Jesus spent a lot of time talking about *money*. He knew money has a way of controlling our hearts (Matthew 6:19–21). Even in Jesus' interaction with the wealthy young ruler (Matthew 19:16–22), the pull of idolatry is apparent as the young man is unable to give up "control" of his stuff. Thus, the scriptural principle is not only to give your time, energy, and talents to gospel efforts but also your finances.

In Scripture, the local church is God's "Plan A" for making disciples of all nations. The apostle Paul in the book of Acts traveled on multiple missionary journeys, making disciples, planting churches, and raising funds for these churches. Why? Because that was God's plan to reach people with the good news of Jesus!

Here are some action points to consider as you give:

- Give in response to the gospel. Jesus gave *everything* for you. Give in response to the gift of salvation, forgiveness, and life that *he* gives.
- Don't give your leftovers. Give what the Bible calls your "firstfruits," your first and best. A practical example of this is to give as soon as you are paid, not *after* all the bills are paid.
- Give sacrificially, cheerfully, and joyfully.
- Start giving immediately. Don't wait! Some insist on giving 10 percent. (The Old Testament called this a "tithe," though debate exists over the exact percentage given by the Israelites.) Some refer to the New Testament standard of giving as "grace giving." If grace abounds above and beyond the law, a good principle is to make 10 percent the "launchpad," or starting point, for your giving.

Biblical Worldview and Witness

A Passage to Dive Into

Read 1 Timothy 1–6 this week.

We recommend reading a chapter each day (Monday–Friday). As you read, ask yourself the following questions:

1. What does this passage reveal about God?
2. What does it reveal about humanity/me?
3. Is there a command of God that I can obey? How can I apply this passage to my life this week? Is there any sin that I need to confess?
4. How does this passage point me to Jesus?

Pointers

- Don't get overwhelmed!
- Pray as you read—ask God to help you understand.
- Highlight what stands out to you.
- If you have questions, write them down!
- As you read, ask if there's something you can apply to your life today.

A Promise to Deposit

*We primarily know Jesus through
the Bible (John 5:39–40).*

In the Introduction, we said:

> Thinking about reading the Bible may be
> overwhelming to you. You may not even know
> where to begin! In fact, some people start in the Old
> Testament but then get discouraged and give up
> after getting a few books in. The Old Testament is
> immensely important, but it ultimately points ahead
> and prepares us for the arrival of Jesus in the New
> Testament. In fact, once you understand the New
> Testament (Matthew–Revelation), then you can
> go back and better understand the purpose of the
> Old Testament.

Want to hear some good news? At this point in your spiritual journey, just in the last eight weeks, you've covered *six* books of the Bible. To put things in perspective, you've read nearly a tenth of the books of the Bible! Let that sink in.

The Bible ("the Word," "Scripture") comprises sixty-six books: thirty-nine Old Testament books and twenty-seven New Testament books.

The Old Testament first gives the story of creation. It tells of humanity failing to bear the image of God. Yet even amid humanity's rebellion, a redemptive God moved toward sinful people to pursue relationship and restoration. It's the story of God's calling Abraham, Isaac, and Jacob (Israel). It's the story of the nation of Israel's journey from Egypt back to the land of Canaan, and ultimately Israel's failure to believe and follow God, which led to their captivity. However, through it all, God was faithful. His forever covenant with his people held fast, and the story of redemption continued into the New Testament.

The New Testament tells the story of Jesus, the fulfillment of the Law and the Prophets (Matthew 5:17). The Gospels reveal the life and teachings of Jesus. The book of Acts then gives us a snapshot of God's mission and movement through the early church. Paul's letters unpack the rich theology around salvation, justification, sanctification (remember these words?) and give us practical handles for our personal lives, work, homes, marriage, and life in biblical community. Other New Testament books expound upon the relationship between faith and works as well as how to persevere through trials and persecution. Finally, the book of Revelation (though at times difficult for *anyone* to understand) gives us a picture of things to come before Jesus returns to the earth.

But what is the main point of reading the Bible? And do you read the Bible once, and then you're done?

Years ago, there was the story of an especially eager new Christian who after reading the Bible exclaimed to the person discipling him (helping him know and follow Jesus): "Okay, I'm done with the Bible. What's next?"

He received the response: "Okay, now you're going to want to read it again."

What? Again? Why would you read the same book over and over again?

The simple answer is this. You read the Bible repeatedly because it's the primary way to know Jesus and grow in your personal relationship with him.

Of course, every Christian is called to know, study, and even *delight* in God's Word, the Bible. In fact, take some time this week or next to read Psalm 119 in one sitting. It's long (the longest psalm recorded), but it will give you a rich, immersive experience of the value and significance of God's Word.

- James 1:22 calls Christians not just to read and hear God's Word but also to apply it—to "do" it!
- Acts 17:10–11 reveals the people of Berea studied the Scriptures to verify the truth of Paul's teaching.
- Paul, in 2 Timothy 2:15, exhorts Christians to "rightly [handle] the word of truth."

Hopefully, you're grasping the picture. The Bible is important! In fact, growing in your biblical worldview is perhaps *the most* important goal right now. Why? Because the pull of the culture is always toward ideologies and idols that point you back to dependence on self, human solutions, and humanity's innate goodness.

Learning to see the world around you
through the lens of Scripture must become
a primary aim of yours moving forward.

Over time (not overnight!), you must strive to grow in a holistic knowledge and understanding of the Bible.

However, this comes with a *warning*. In Jesus' time, the Jewish "Bible experts" ultimately arrested, tortured, and crucified their promised Messiah (Jesus). But how could this happen? How did they miss it, even though they had devoted their lives to studying the Old Testament?

Perhaps Jesus said it best in John 5:39–40: "You search the Scriptures because you think that in them you have eternal life; and it is they that bear witness about me, yet you refuse to come to me that you may have life." And herein lies an important reminder: the Bible is not the *end* but the *means* by which you know and follow Jesus. Never forget that Jesus is the source of your life.

If you find yourself getting geeked out with knowledge or puffed up with pride in your study of the Bible, this should serve as a warning. If your love for Jesus (and others!) is not growing, and your life and character are not reflecting Jesus, consider it a giant red flag that you have gotten offtrack and veered into dangerous territory in your spiritual journey. Come back to Jesus—not a Jesus of your own imagination or making. Come back to the Jesus of Scripture. But let your steadfast focus on the Bible never lead you away from the steadfast love of your Savior.

A Truth to Discover

The Bible is fully sufficient for the Christ follower.

All Scripture is breathed out by God
and profitable for teaching, for reproof,
for correction, and for training in righteousness, that the man of God may be complete, equipped for every good work.

2 Timothy 3:16–17

When we talk about the "sufficiency of Scripture," it's important to qualify the phrase! If Scripture is "sufficient," does that mean you can plumb the depths of quantum mechanics in its pages? Can you discover a detailed discussion on the webbed design of the duck-billed platypus's feet? Does the Bible reveal anything about the technological benefits (versus downfalls) of overusing Alexa, Google, and Siri? The obvious answer to all these questions is unequivocally no. So what does it mean that the Bible is "sufficient"?

Question 3 of the Westminster Shorter Catechism gives us some insight:

What do the Scriptures principally teach?

The Scriptures principally teach what man is to believe concerning God and what duty God requires of man.[11]

Further, Ligonier Ministries tells us:

> According to the Reformation—and biblical—
> principle of sola Scriptura, Scripture is the only
> infallible rule of faith for the church. Because
> the Word of God is the only *theopneustos*—God-
> breathed—special revelation that we possess today
> (2 Tim. 3:16), then no rule of faith can supersede
> Scripture. There is no higher court to which we can
> appeal for faith and practice, for there is nowhere
> else besides Scripture where we can surely find God's
> voice today. That God's Word is inspired does not
> mean that He dictated it or that He overrode the
> personalities, gifts, and stylistic choices of the human
> authors through whom the written Word of God
> has come to us. It does mean that He worked in and
> through these authors such that their words are His
> words. Sola Scriptura also leads us to the doctrine of
> biblical sufficiency. To say that Scripture is sufficient
> is to say that the Bible contains all that we need for
> determining what we must believe and how we are to
> live before God. Scripture must be interpreted if we
> are to understand what we are to believe and how we
> are to act, but the sufficiency of Scripture indicates
> that we need no other source of special revelation for
> faith and life in addition to the Bible.[12]

We have affirmed the authority of the Bible as well as
its sufficiency. But at this point, we also must affirm the

absolute inerrancy of the Bible, which includes striving for clarity of the phrase "the inerrancy of Scripture."

Though we do not have the original manuscripts of the Old Testament and New Testament, we have *thousands* of both partial and complete copies of the Bible, including some manuscripts of the New Testament that date to within a generation or two of Jesus. On the standard of manuscript evidence alone, the Bible is far and away the most historically reliable book of antiquity. Now this doesn't remove the element of faith, but it should inspire and ignite confidence in the life of the Christ follower.

Though a bit lengthy (so bear with it!), the Chicago Statement on Biblical Inerrancy is very helpful:

> God, who is Himself Truth and speaks truth only, has inspired Holy Scripture in order thereby to reveal Himself to lost mankind through Jesus Christ as Creator and Lord, Redeemer and Judge. Holy Scripture is God's witness to Himself. Holy Scripture, being God's own Word, written by men prepared and superintended by His Spirit, is of infallible divine authority in all matters upon which it touches: it is to be believed, as God's instruction, in all that it affirms; obeyed, as God's command, in all that it requires; embraced, as God's pledge, in all that it promises. The Holy Spirit, Scripture's divine Author, both authenticates it to us by His inward witness and opens our minds to understand its meaning. Being wholly and verbally God-given,

> Scripture is without error or fault in all its teaching, no less in what it states about God's acts in creation, about the events of world history, and about its own literary origins under God, than in its witness to God's saving grace in individual lives. The authority of Scripture is inescapably impaired if this total divine inerrancy is in any way limited, disregarded, or made relative to a view of truth contrary to the Bible's own; and such lapses bring serious loss to both the individual and the Church.[13]

Though this is all useful information, let's pause to talk about the practical implications. Know that the pull of the world is always toward something "more" and "new." (See Acts 17:16–34 and Paul's interaction with the people of Athens.)

Humanity's insatiable appetite for "higher knowledge" and "new revelation" inevitably leads to people seeking to be the standard and arbiter of truth. Because of this, truth becomes relative—to the situation, to the culture, and to the opinions and whims of people.

In the twenty-first century, you can see this all around you in a culture that rejects the absolute truth of a sovereign God. Christians should know this battle isn't a "new" one (after all, Solomon said nothing is new under the sun in Ecclesiastes 1:9), but that doesn't mean the pull and power of culture aren't pervasive as it relentlessly lures us into a world of relativism, doubt, and, ultimately, despair.

Why despair? Because if truth is relative and the solution lies within humanity, people would have long ago self-actualized and figured out how to live at peace within themselves and with the world around them. So the problem is not insufficient knowledge; rather, the issue is a problem of the will. Our sinful human hearts don't want God apart from his intervention (and now we come full circle back to Week 1!). Only through the revealed Word of God is our rebellion and unbelief exposed for what it is (sin). Only through the Scriptures can we truly understand the incredible scope of God's redemption and restoration in Jesus.

Always remember:

- The Bible is sufficient.
- Jesus is enough.
- Against the pull of "more" and "new," allow yourself to be satisfied in Jesus alone.

As Paul encourages us: "See to it that no one takes you captive by philosophy and empty deceit, according to human tradition, according to the elemental spirits of the world, and not according to Christ" (Colossians 2:8).

Discussion

1. Talk with the one who is walking with you through *Christ Rhythms* about the balance of being Bible-centered, while also not missing the point that the Bible is meant to draw you into a deeper relationship

with Jesus. (Remember, the Bible is the *means*, not the *end*.)

_____

_____

_____

_____

2. Do you have any questions about what it means to live with a "biblical worldview"? How can the sufficiency and inerrancy of Scripture inspire and ignite confidence in your life? Where have you felt the pull of culture toward relativism, doubt, and despair?

_____

_____

_____

_____

3. Do you have any questions about 2 Timothy 3:16–17? Do you have any questions about this truth to discover?

_____

_____

_____

_____

A Habit to Develop: Witness

*Read Romans 1:16; Acts 1:8;
1 Peter 3:15; Colossians 4:5-6. Discuss the importance
of a Christian witness.*

An intricate connection exists between the Word and our witness. When the Word of God fills our hearts and minds, the Word will overflow in our lives through our witness.

In Christianity, we use the term "witness" as a synonym for sharing the gospel with others, especially those who do not have a personal relationship with Jesus. Though the primary element in our witness should be the Bible, witnessing can also encompass sharing our own personal testimony of what God has done in our lives and how Jesus has changed us.

Here are some practical action steps to consider as you witness:

- Remember that you're sharing the Word of God, and the gospel is powerful and primary. Though you can share your personal story of how God changed you, be sure to use the Bible.
- The best balance to strike is one of courage and grace. Be bold to share truth. But don't be a "jerk for

117

Jesus." Unfortunately, the world has far too many of these!

- Remember that the Holy Spirit is your source of power. Rely on him not only to give you the courage but also the right words and the right opportunities to share the gospel.

- Remember that God saves, not you. Your role is to be a faithful messenger. There is God's role, your role, and the role of the person with whom you are sharing. You can't play all three roles!

- Trust that God is drawing others to himself and pray for receptive hearts to the gospel.

- Finally, don't wait until you're a Bible expert to be a witness. God is far more concerned with your level of biblical obedience than your level of biblical knowledge. That's not to say you shouldn't strive to know the Scriptures well, but you must be faithful with what you already know. Start there!

Conclusion

Congratulations on completing the *Christ Rhythms* journey! But this is just the beginning! This book is only meant to be a jumpstart. Imagine coming across someone stranded in a parking lot or on the side of the road. Now, picture a good Samaritan coming along with jumper cables to help jumpstart their vehicle. If you were looking on and heard the engine turn over and roar to life, you would expect the recipient of the jumpstart to put their car in gear and continue down the road. How strange it would be if they simply idled in the same place, in their fully functioning car. How strange it would be if they *stopped* after the jumpstart!

Over the course of eight weeks, you have read the Word of God.

You have taken to heart promises from God's Word.

You have received a crash-course on some basic yet essential theology (truth about God).

Finally, you've also begun to put into practice consequential Christian habits that will help you know and follow Jesus.

Don't be content to be idle. Plan to read the remainder of the New Testament. Find a few Christians who know and love you, who can hold you accountable to continuing in these "Christ rhythms." Share with others what Jesus is doing in your heart and life. Be encouraged! God has an incredible plan and purpose for your life "in Christ." Continue to press into God's calling and mission. Know that he is at work within you and all around you for his glory.

> God has an incredible plan and purpose for your life "in Christ."

One final thought in light of Jesus' command to "go therefore and make disciples of all nations" (Matthew 28:19). Who is one person you could disciple (as you have been discipled)? Perhaps you have a friend, neighbor, coworker, family member, or classmate with whom you could walk through *Christ Rhythms* and help them jumpstart their discipleship journey. Take the bold step of reaching out and inviting them into the eight-week process.

Keep going.

Keep pursuing Jesus.

You've got this.

More importantly, God has you!

Notes

1. Tim Keller, *The Meaning of Marriage: Facing the Complexities of Commitment with the Wisdom of God* (New York: Penguin, 2011), 44.

2. Wayne Grudem, *Systematic Theology: An Introduction to Biblical Doctrine* (Grand Rapids: Zondervan, 1994), 723.

3. Warren Wiersbe, *The Bible Exposition Commentary* (Colorado Springs: Victor, 2001), 532. (Note: In his commentary on Romans 6, Wiersbe speaks specifically about how the death of Jesus paid the penalty for sin and broke the power of sin.)

4. R. C. Sproul, "What Is Imputed Righteousness?" Ligonier Ministries, accessed June 15, 2021, ligonier.org/learn/qas/what-is-imputed-righteousness. (Note: This transcript is from an Ask R. C. Live event with R. C. Sproul and was lightly edited for readability.)

5. *Merriam-Webster*, s.v. "identity (*n.*)," accessed June 25, 2021, merriam-webster.com/dictionary/identity.

6. R. C. Sproul, *Who Is the Holy Spirit?* (Sanford, FL: Reformation Trust, 2012), 36.

7. Steven D. Brooks, *Worship Quest: An Exploration of Worship Leadership* (Eugene: Wipf and Stock, 2015), 166. (Note: Brooks quotes Warren Wiersbe as he explores various definitions of worship.)

8. D. A. Carson, *Worship by the Book* (Grand Rapids: Zondervan, 2002), 37.

9. *Merriam-Webster*, s.v. "sovereignty (*n.*)," accessed July 20, 2021, merriam-webster.com/dictionary/sovereignty.

10. "Sovereign over Our Steps," Ligonier Ministries, accessed August 1, 2021, ligonier.org/learn/devotionals/sovereign-over-our-steps.

11. "Shorter Catechism: Text and Scripture Proofs," The Westminster Standard, accessed August 10, 2021, thewestminsterstandard.org/westminster-shorter-cate-chism/#1.

12. "Biblical Sufficiency," Ligonier Ministries, accessed August 10, 2021, ligonier.org/learn/devotionals/bibli-cal-sufficiency.

13. "The Chicago Statement on Biblical Inerrancy," The Gospel Coalition, accessed August 10, 2021, thegospelco-alition.org/themelios/article/the-chicago-statement-on-bib-lical-inerrancy/.

About the Author

JONATHAN BROOKS serves as the lead pastor of Restoration Church Bryan in Bryan, Texas. He is a graduate of Dallas Theological Seminary and Texas A&M University. Jonathan lives in Bryan with his wife, Stephani, and their five children.